Respect

BY CYNTHIA AMOROSO

Published by The Child's World®
1980 Lookout Drive • Mankato, MN 56003-1705
800-599-READ • www.childsworld.com

Acknowledgments
The Child's World®: Mary Berendes, Publishing Director
The Design Lab: Design
Pamela J. Mitsakos: Photo Research
Christine Florie: Editing

Photographs ©: David M. Budd Photography: 5, 9, 11, 13, 15, 17, 21;
iStockphoto.com/Gerville: cover, 1; iStockphoto.com/Jani Bryson Studios,
Inc.: 7; iStockphoto.com/sjlocke/digital planet design: 19.

ISBN 9781623235246
LCCN 2013931452

Printed in the United States of America
Mankato, MN
July, 2013
PA02172

ABOUT THE AUTHOR

Cynthia Amoroso is Director of Curriculum and Instruction for a school district in Minnesota. She enjoys reading, writing, gardening, traveling, and spending time with friends and family.

Table of Contents

What Is Respect?

When you respect people, you treat them well. You **consider** their needs and feelings. You are careful about what you do and say to them. You are fair to them. You treat them as you would like to be treated.

Showing respect means making sure everyone gets a fair chance.

Respecting Others

You know that good manners are important. You say "please" and "thank you." You talk quietly when you are in a library. You do not yell at people. You do not bother people when they are busy. Using good manners shows respect for the people around you.

You can respect others in a library by whispering.

Respect at School

Your teacher asks another student a question.

You know the answer! You raise your hand. Your teacher waits for the other student to answer. You show respect by being quiet and **patient**. You let the other student answer.

Waiting your turn shows respect for others.

Respecting Other People's Things

Your sister has a special game. You love to play it!

She lets you use it when she is gone. When you are

done, you put it away. You are careful not to lose

any pieces. You show respect for your sister by being

careful with her game.

You can show respect by taking good care of people's things.

Respecting Other People's Needs

Your brother does his homework in the kitchen. He needs quiet time to do a good job. You and a friend feel like playing. You would like to use the kitchen table. But you respect your brother's needs. You play in another room instead.

Paying attention to other people's needs shows respect.

13

Respecting Other People's Homes

You are playing ball in your yard. The ball bounces into your neighbor's garden. Your neighbor loves to work in her garden. She works hard to make her flowers grow. You could stomp through quickly to get your ball. But you step carefully. You respect your neighbor. You are careful not to harm her garden.

Being careful can be a way of showing respect.

Respecting Your Parents

Your parents want you to keep your room clean. They want you to set the table for meals. They have rules you need to follow. You do not always want to do these things. You show respect for your parents by following their rules.

Following rules shows respect for the people who made them.

Respecting Your Country

You go to a baseball game. Before it begins, the nation's **anthem** is played. You stop talking to your friends. You place your hand over your heart. You look at the flag and sing along. It feels good to show respect for your flag and country. Showing respect for your country is called **patriotism**.

There are lots of ways to show respect for your country.

Showing Respect Helps Everyone

Respecting others makes them feel good. It also makes them think kindly of you. It makes you feel good, too. When you respect others, they will respect you in return. That helps everybody get along better!

Showing respect is a great way to show that you care!

Glossary

anthem–An anthem is a national song. The anthem of the United States is "The Star-Spangled Banner."

consider–If you consider something, you think about it carefully.

patient–Being patient means waiting for something without getting upset.

patriotism–Patriotism is a feeling of love and respect for your country.

Learn More

Books

Cook, Julia. *My Mouth Is a Volcano!* Chattanooga, TN: National Center for Youth Issues, 2005.

Meiners, Cheri J. *Respect and Take Care of Things.* Minneapolis, MN: Free Spirit, 2004.

Thomas, Pat. *Everyone Matters: A First Look at Respect for Others.* Hauppauge, NY: Barron's Educational Series, 2010.

Web Sites

Visit our Web site for links about respect: childsworld.com/links

Note to Parents, Teachers, and Librarians: We routinely verify our Web links to make sure they are safe and active sites. So encourage your readers to check them out!

Index